Avalanche!

THE DEADLY SLIDE

Jane Duden

Perfection Learning® Corporation

Cover Photo: Digital Stock
Inside Illustration: Mike Aspengren, Kay Ewald

About the Author

Jane Duden is a former elementary teacher in Minnesota and Germany. As a freelance writer, Ms. Duden has written 31 nonfiction books for children. She writes for teachers and kids on many topics, but her favorites are animals, science, and the environment. Her quest for stories and adventures has taken her to every continent, including Antarctica. At home in Minneapolis, she likes cooking, swimming, biking, in-line skating, and playing with her pets. Best of all, she likes visits from her grown-up daughter, who is away at college.

Acknowledgments

Special thanks to Dale Atkins of the Colorado Avalanche Information Center for assistance in preparation of the manuscript and to Lester Morlang, Liam Fitzgerald, Steve Conger, and Doug Abromeit for personal interviews.

Image credits: Art Today pp. 5, 47, 52 (top); Patrick Cone pp. 10, 22, 26, 29, 40, 44, 49, 50; Corbis/Bettmann p. 43; Corel pp. 11, 16, 24, 36, 37, 38, 51, 52 (middle and bottom); Digital Stock pp. 3, 4, 7, 19, 23, 27, 28, 30, 33, 41, 46

Table of Contents

Chapter

Avalanche at Snowstorm Peak

SUNDAY, NOVEMBER 17, 1985. Jack Ritter did not know it would be his last day alive. Lester Morlang had no idea about the disaster ahead. The men were at their gold mine, the Bessey G. It was high in the Colorado mountains.

The mine had two portals (doorways). One was on the west side of the mountain. But the men were at the east portal. There were no roads on this side. No people for miles.

It was nearly 6 p.m. A **blizzard** was brewing. Snowstorm Peak loomed above. Its slopes were heavy with snow.

This was **avalanche** country. An avalanche is a crashing, sudden river of snow. But the miners thought they'd have warning. They could duck inside the mine.

The men switched on the lights on their miner's hats. They were building a roof over the old east portal. The roof would keep snow away. Jack ran a small diesel-powered loader on treads. Lester stood in the bucket. The loader lifted the bucket

to roof level. Lester put a timber into place. Then—*avalanche!* The men never saw or heard it coming. And so began the struggle to survive.

BURIED ALIVE!

The avalanche began right at the mine. Suddenly megatons of snow covered Jack. It flipped Lester out of the bucket and **buried** him. The snow sped on down the canyon. It ran over anything in its path.

Lester's body was locked under tons of snow. He knew he must dig out. Or he would die in a tomb of ice. Is this what it's like to die? he thought in panic.

Lester was buried with his hands in front of his face. That was lucky. His hands formed a tiny air pocket. Wiggling his fingers made more space to breathe. Could he dig out more space ahead?

He could hear the loader running. He called to Jack. But yelling made him lose his breath. So Lester made himself breathe slowly. This kept him from inhaling the light, feathery snow.

Lester thought about his wife and son. He sent thoughts to his dad, asking for help. He prayed. He made up his mind to live.

He grabbed a fistful of snow and pulled it toward his chest. Then another. And another. Straining every muscle, he pushed with his elbows. He moved ahead a few inches!

On he dug. After a while, the loader quit. Now there was dead silence. Sick with fear, Lester hoped Jack was safe. Maybe Jack had dug back in the mine and gone for help. But who could help them? There was nobody for miles.

Lester clawed at the snow. He wriggled like a caterpillar. Cramps twisted his stomach. His hands were frozen. His muscles hurt. He rested. Then he clawed some more.

Ten hours passed. Then 15. The lamp on Lester's miner's hat still shone. He saw only an endless white blank. Without the light, everything went black. He thought of his family. He would NOT give up!

STILL TRAPPED

Then, after 22 hours, Lester turned off his lamp again. And this time he saw light! It was now about 4:00 Monday afternoon. He soon broke his way to freedom, leaping with joy. Lester Morlang had dug through 30 feet of snow!

But Lester's ordeal was not over. His hands were numb. It was freezing outside. A blizzard was raging. And it would soon be dark. He was still trapped on the mountain.

Lester tried to stamp out HELP in the snow. But the wind blew snow over the letters. He used his hard hat for a scoop to make the end of the tunnel into a snow cave. He huddled inside for the night.

Meanwhile, the sheriff was just getting the news. Jack Ritter's son had found the mine's east portal blocked with snow. He had seen no sign of his dad or Lester Morlang. The sheriff's heart sank. Most buried avalanche victims are alive after 15

minutes. After 30 minutes, less than half are alive. By now, a day had passed. Outside, a blizzard blew fiercely. No one could get there tonight. The search would have to wait until daylight.

In his snow cave, Lester waited. He jammed his frozen hands into his armpits. During the night, a second avalanche came. But the snow raced over the top of the cave. Scared to death, Lester counted. He thought about his family. He prayed for all he was worth.

THE SEARCH

At daybreak Tuesday, the rescue effort began. Strong winds drove the windchill to 50 degrees below zero. A helicopter flew over the mine. The crew flew low. They looked for clues. A hat, a boot, a glove. But all they saw was snow. If only they could land at the east portal. But it was too steep and windy.

There was danger of another avalanche. So the pilot got permission to make the snow stable. That meant setting off bombs. The bombs started thundering rivers of snow. Now the slopes were safe for rescuers to search.

Powerful snowplows started up the roads. Another helicopter brought searchers. One was Lester's father. He awoke in the night, thinking that he heard Lester calling to him, telling him he was cold. Mr. Morlang felt certain that his son was alive.

The helicopter landed at the west portal. The searchers waded through the mine's long tunnel. Then they came out the east portal. Shoveling into the snow, they soon found Jack Ritter. His frozen body lay by the loader.

DOWN THE MOUNTAIN

Lester was again digging out. He knew he had to follow the mine safety plan. Get down to Junction Creek. Go to the first farmhouse.

Lester heard a roaring in the sky. It was a helicopter! He waved frantically. But it did not see him. It sped beyond the ridge, up to the mine.

Then Lester heard the explosions. He knew they were meant to start avalanches. Lester was right in the path! He scrambled behind a big tree. The tree kept the rumbling snow away. When it was over, Lester stepped out onto new hard-packed snow. It was 15 to 20 feet deep. He was angry. But the rescue team had no way of knowing he was down there.

He had to keep going. Sliding and falling, Lester went forward. The snow was like concrete. If the avalanche had carried him down there, he could never have dug out. At last, Lester reached the bottom of the **avalanche path**. Now he faced deep powder snow. He had to pack the snow five or six times just to take each step. If he didn't, he'd sink to his chest in snow.

Lester tells the rest of the story. "Just before dark, the searchers took one more run. This time they flew over the path of our mine safety plan. The sheriff knew the plan.

"I was already past the hard pack and back into the soft snow. I heard the copter. I held up my hands. They saw me!

"The ravine was narrow. Not much wider than the copter blades. I knew at any time the next avalanche could come. The copter hovered. I climbed up on a big snow-covered rock. The pilot came down close enough so I could grab the skid on the helicopter. I was hanging on with my elbow. When I jumped on, the engine stalled in the narrow, tight spot. I yelled 'Go, go, go!' They got me inside. They told me, 'You're a miracle!' "

THE MIRACLE MAN OF SNOWSTORM PEAK

"I'd seen plenty of avalanches," says Lester. "I never really was scared of them. Today I still ride snowmobiles. But I know a good place and a bad place. Jack Ritter was wise about that. We were pushing it. We knew it was going to avalanche again on that old side of the mine. We were building that little porch overhang so the snow would run off it.

"After the avalanche, I talked to a lot of experts. You have to know the type of snow, the time of day. You can tell where an avalanche is going to be. They have their paths through the year.

"I feel really lucky. I lost only the tip of one finger. I couldn't walk for a long time. I was in bed for weeks. My feet were numb. It took a year of therapy. I had to learn how to get my balance and how to walk again. The love and support of Anita and Benji helped the months go faster.

"We've always been a tight family. But the avalanche made everything tighter. Some days I just stop and remember. Then just the simplest thing can be so grand."

Lester is no longer a miner. He owns gravel trucks and does custom hauling. He put up a memorial for his partner at the mine. And he named the west portal after Jack Ritter—*The J.R. Portal*. As for Lester, he is the Miracle Man of Snowstorm Peak.

Chapter 2

White Death

An avalanche is a mass of snow moving down a slope. It's also called a **snowslide.** Ice, dirt, rocks, trees, or other junk may be in the snow. When it all comes to rest, it's called **avalanche debris.**

No one expects tragedy when out for sport or fun. But unstable snow is a huge danger. The power of snow can snuff

out life. An avalanche can come with no warning. Riding snow in the mountains means risking your life.

An avalanche can race at 200 miles an hour or more. It can crash with 50 tons of force per square yard. Not all avalanches are large. Not all are fast-moving. But whatever the speed, it's too fast for anyone in the way. Avalanches are White Death.

Avalanches are natural. The world has perhaps a million avalanches per year.

Avalanches can happen on any steep, snow-covered slope. The steeper the slope, the faster the slide. Most avalanches are not a problem. Not unless people or their property are in the way. Mountains, snow, and people can add up to fun. Sadly, they are also the ingredients for an avalanche.

Even small avalanches are deadly. They can smash buildings and snap trees. They can bury and kill people too. Children have been caught in snowslides while sledding. It happened to three boys in Montana in 1985. They were ages seven to nine. One boy was killed. Even young children can learn what makes an avalanche. And everyone can stay away from steep slopes right after a storm.

In the United States, an average of 24 people die in avalanches each year. That's more than die in hurricanes. It's more than die in earthquakes.

In Canada, 97 people died in avalanches between 1979 and 1994. All but two were killed while enjoying fun activities.

Between 1985 and 1991, Europe had more than 700 deaths in 12 countries. These numbers are only the deaths. Hundreds of injuries go unreported.

Avalanche Fatalities in the World 1992–1998

	92–93	93–94	94–95	95–96	96–97	97–98	Total
France	23	23	23	44	23	35	171
U.S.A.	29	13	28	30	22	26	148
Austria	23	13	24	37	27	11	135
Switzerland	28	21	20	17	24	13	123
Italy	24	24	12	10	13	14	97
Canada	9	8	15	9	14	23	78
Norway	1	5	3	2	4	6	21
Poland	1	1	0	5	5	2	14
Spain	2	0	6	2	4	0	14
Germany	3	1	1	3	4	0	12
Slovenia	0	0	1	6	0	1	8

Colorado Avalanche Information Center

WHEN PEOPLE GET CAUGHT

Most avalanche deaths happen while people are out for sport or fun. People are skiing. Snowmobiling. Ice climbing. Snowshoeing. Or snowboarding.

Sometimes, people are killed in avalanches while working. Some victims are miners, like Jack Ritter. Some are construction workers. Or power company workers. Some are driving in cars or trucks. Some are volunteer rescuers. Ski patrollers have died in avalanches while at work. So have snowplow drivers and photographers.

Most avalanche victims are in their 20s. In the past five years, snowmobilers led the list of victims. Now snowboarding is getting more popular. That means more snowboarders may die in avalanches.

Winter recreation is booming. Avalanche deaths in the U.S. are going up. More people use the **backcountry** for sports. Snow machines carry people faster and higher. Skiers, snowboarders, and climbers get more skillful. Sometimes they push the limits.

In the United States, most avalanche accidents happen in Colorado. The reason is its climate. This state has a thinner snow cover and colder temperatures than other mountain states. The two are a deadly combination for a weak, dangerous **snowpack.** But more people are moving into the mountains. So accidents in the other mountain states are catching up.

When are avalanches most likely? During snowstorms and during thaws. In Colorado, about 2,000 avalanches are reported in a normal winter. More than 80 percent occur during or just after large snowstorms. February has the most avalanches. Then March, then January. Most avalanches caused by thaw are in April.

U.S. Avalanche Fatalities by Activity 1992–1998

		92–93	93–94	94–95	95–96	96–97	97–98	Total
R E C R E A T I O N	Climbers	3	2	6	9	6	3	29
	Backcountry skiers	9	2	7	6	0	0	24
	In-area skiers	0	0	0	0	0	0	0
	Out-of-bounds skiers	5	0	0	1	0	1	7
	Backcountry snowboarders	2	0	1	3	1	4	11
	Out-of-bounds snowboarders	1	0	2	1	0	0	4
	Snowmobilers	2	9	7	5	6	14	43
	Misc. recreation	4	0	1	2	7	4	18
W O R K	Patrollers	1	0	1	1	0	0	3
	Motorists/ highway workers	1	0	1	0	0	0	2
	Residents	0	0	2	1	0	0	3

Colorado Avalanche Information Center

United States Avalanche Fatalities 1992–1998

	92–93	93–94	94–95	95–96	96–97	97–98	Total
Colorado	12	1	9	7	1	6	36
Alaska	7	2	6	8	4	3	30
Montana	1	6	3	3	1	7	21
Utah	3	1	5	2	6	2	19
Idaho	2	0	0	3	3	3	11
Wyoming	1	1	1	3	2	1	9
Washington	0	0	1	0	5	2	8
California	1	0	2	0	1	1	5
Oregon	1	2	0	0	0	1	4
New Hampshire	0	0	0	3	0	0	3
New York	1	0	0	0	0	0	1
Arizona	0	0	1	0	0	0	1
New Mexico	0	0	0	1	0	0	1

Colorado Avalanche Information Center

A SNOWBOARDER WHO SURVIVED

Steven Koch is a great snowboarder. He has even snowboarded on Mt. Kilimanjaro in Africa. He planned a new run. It was on Wyoming's Mt. Owen. No snowboarder had ever done that.

Steven was on his way to the top of a ridge. He was alone. There he planned to check out the route. He would look for dangers. But he didn't quite make it to the top. *Avalanche!*

It rushed over a ledge above him. Like wet cement, it hit him full force. It knocked him on his back. It ripped off his backpack.

Steven tumbled about 20 seconds. He slid 2,200 feet. The snow battered him. Both knees were badly injured. His face was bruised and scratched. His ribs and lungs were hurt. It was hard for him to breathe.

He dragged himself off the path to a safe spot. He rested. Time passed. The warm sun cooled. He was in pain and needed help. He rolled onto his back. Then he used his elbows to push. He moved crablike through the wet snow. Finally, he had to stop. When Steven did not come back that night, his friends called the rescue rangers.

The next day, a helicopter rescued Steven. He took months to recover. But he is back on the slopes again. Steven was lucky.

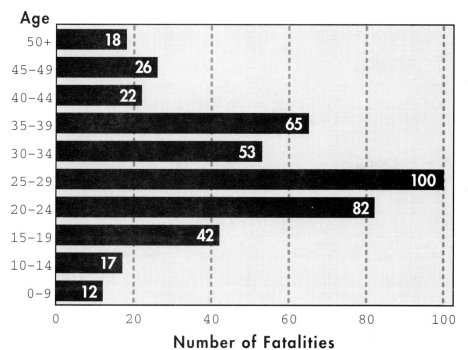

United States Avalanche Fatalities by Age
1950/51 to 1996/97   Colorado Avalanche Information Center

Mountain Snow: The Snowpack

Snow is made of tiny ice crystals. When they form in the **atmosphere,** they **bond** together. This creates snowflakes.

It snows a lot in the mountains. As snowflakes build up on slopes, they form layers. Snow on the ground is called *snowpack*. The snowpack builds layer by layer each time it snows.

Each tiny snow grain bonds to other snow grains. Grains bond inside the snow layer. Some layers are strong. Some are weak. The bonds between layers can also be strong or weak. Strong and weak layers are caused by the shape of the snow crystals. Weather also affects the strength of the layers. As weather changes, the snowpack changes. The snowpack is a record of the winter's weather.

Strong snow is not the same as stable snow. Poor bonding between layers makes unstable snow.

A steep slope and unstable snow are deadly. When a stronger layer forms on top of a weaker one and the angle of the slope is steep enough, the snowpack becomes unstable. An entire hillside can break loose. Millions of pounds of snow crash down the slope. Then, watch out!

PARTS OF AN AVALANCHE

All avalanches run in a path. The **starting zone** is where the unstable snow or ice breaks loose. It breaks and starts to slide. Some **avalanche tracks** may have many starting zones. A track is the path where the snow slides. The **runout zone** is where the snow slows and stops.

The debris in a runout zone is heavy. A cubic yard can weigh almost 1,000 pounds. All the debris can weigh millions of pounds.

Picture the snow pushed into a driveway by a snowplow. The longer it sits, the harder it gets. Snow in the runout zone is as hard as concrete.

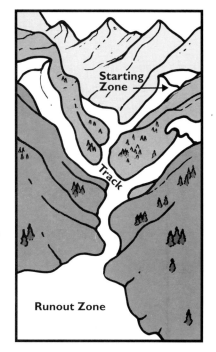

AVALANCHES: ALL SHAPES AND SIZES

Avalanches come in all shapes and sizes. Even a small one can harm or kill if people or property is in its way. What are some types of avalanches?

LOOSE SNOWSLIDES. Loose-snow avalanches break out from a small area. Then they fan out. They pick up more snow as they go. They may come during or after a snowstorm. Warm sunshine can start them. Rain can start them.

SLAB AVALANCHES. Slabs are a layer or layers of well-bonded snow that break away in a hunk. The slab breaks into smaller chunks as it slides.

Slabs can be small or large. They can be hard or soft, wet or dry. High winds are a factor. Winds load slopes with added surface snow. This creates slabs. Most are **triggered** by human activity.

17

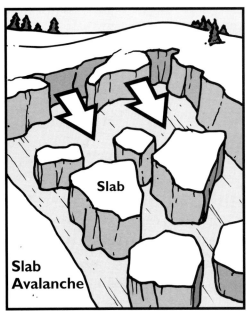

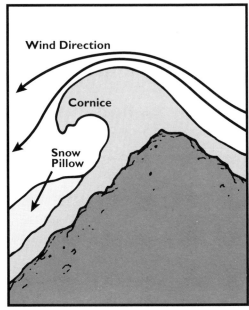

Slab avalanches are the most deadly. The victim has nowhere to run. A slab avalanche killed Jack Ritter. It buried Lester Morlang.

CORNICE AVALANCHES. A **cornice** forms when wind blows snow to a ridge. The snow builds out like a shelf. Cornices are the "bombs" of the backcountry. A cornice "bomb" may hit the snow pillow below. Then a big avalanche starts.

FEBRUARY 1, 1997. WEST MOUNTAIN, IDAHO. Three snowmobilers were ***high marking.*** High marking is a contest. Riders see whose machine can make tracks highest on the slope. The snowmobilers were right below a large cornice. A second driver went way up. He was just under the cornice, on the snow pillow. Then he headed back down the mountain. But his ride triggered an avalanche. It caught him. His snowmobile hit the top of a tree. He was launched downhill in front of the machine. When the snow stopped moving, he was dead.

WHERE DO AVALANCHES OCCUR?

Most avalanches are in the backcountry—outside developed ski areas.

Most skiers go there for thrills, not dangers. But they like to set their own rules. Some like to set their own pace. They may push their luck a little too far. But luck isn't enough. Survival depends on learning where and why avalanches happen.

Most avalanches start on slopes with angles of 30 to 45 degrees. Most are on slopes above **timberline.** And most are on slopes that face away from winds. These are called *leeward slopes.* Such slopes collect snow blowing from the windward sides of ridges. But avalanches can run on small slopes below timberline. Gullies, road cuts, and small openings in the trees are examples. People have even been buried and killed by snow avalanching off a cabin roof.

1997–99* U.S. & CANADA AVALANCHE VICTIMS

DATE	PLACE	DEATHS	DETAILS
4/29/99	Wrangell-St. Elias National Park, AK	1	1 climber caught and killed
4/27/99	Mount McGinnis, Alaska	2	2 backcountry snowboarders partly buried and killed
4/16/99	Talkeetna Mountains, Alaska	1	1 snowmobiler buried and killed
4/15/99	Cordova, Alaska	1	1 construction worker buried and killed
4/7/99	Near Ophir, Colorado	1	1 skier caught, buried, and killed
4/3/99	Chugach Mtns., S. of Eureka, AK	1	1 snowmobiler caught, buried, and killed
3/21/99	Spring Canyon, near Coalville, Utah	0	1 snowmobiler caught, leg broken
3/21/99	Turnagain Pass, Alaska	6	6 snowmobilers caught, buried, and killed
3/21/99	Powerline Pass, Chugach St. Pk., AK	0	3 snowmobilers caught, 2 buried
3/15/99	Rainbow Mountain, near Whistler, BC	0	1 heli-ski guide caught, buried, and injured
3/12/99	Alyeska Ski Resort, Alaska	0	2 skiers caught and partially buried in large slide
3/6/99	Arasta Creek, Gravelly Range, MT	0	2 snowmobilers caught; 1 buried, blue, and very lucky
2/27/99	Kokanee Provincial Park, BC	0	3 backcountry skiers caught and injured
2/20/99	Portneuf Rng. Caribou Natl. For., ID	0	1 skier caught and injured
2/14/99	Near Mt. Baker, Washington	2	1 snowboarder dead; 1 skier caught, buried; still missing and presumed dead
2/10/99	Hailey, Idaho	0	Park damaged, deer herd killed
2/9/99	Town of Hailey, Idaho	0	3 houses damaged by avalanche
2/6/99	Lone Peak Area, Utah	1	1 snowshoer caught, buried, and killed
2/6/99	Cumberland Pass, Colorado	3	4 caught; 1 partly buried, 3 buried and killed (2 skiers, 1 snowmobiler)
2/6/99	Lake Mary area, California	1	3 caught; 1 buried and killed
1/30/99	Grand Mesa, Colorado	1	1 snowmobiler caught, buried, and killed
1/29/99	East side of Mount Nebo, Utah	1	1 snowmobiler caught, buried, and killed
1/29/99	Blue Mountains, Oregon	1	1 snowboarder caught, buried, and killed
1/27/99	Grouse Mtn., near Vancouver, BC	1	5 hikers caught; 4 injured, 1 missing & presumed dead
1/23/99	MacAtee Basin, Big Sky, MT	0	snowmobiler survived
1/22/99	Aspen Highlands Ski Area, Colorado	1	2 out-of-bounds skiers; 1 caught, buried, and killed
1/19/99	Casper Bowl, Jackson Hole, WY	1	1 snowboarder swept over 300' cliff and killed
1/18/99	Near Mt. Baker, Washington	1	1 snowboarder caught, buried; still missing and presumed dead
1/14/99	Near Lake Louise, Alberta	1	2 skiers caught; 1 buried and killed
1/7/99	Terrace, British Columbia	2	2 avalanche technicians caught, buried, and killed
1/5/99	Tri-County Peak, Park City, Utah	0	2 skiers caught and buried; 3 skiers fired and cited
1/4/99	Togwotee Pass, Wyoming	1	1 snowmobiler caught, buried, and killed
1/2/99	Southeast of Fairview, Utah	2	2 snowboarders caught and killed
1/1/99	N. Quebec, Kangiqsualujjuaq, QB	9	school gym with 500 people inside; 9 killed, 25 injured
1/1/99	Beaverhead Mountains, Montana	0	2 snowmobilers caught, not buried, not injured
12/30/98	Bitterroot Mountains, Montana	1	1 snowmobiler/shoveler caught, buried, and killed
12/24/98	Cypress Mountain, BC	1	1 snowboarder caught, buried, and killed
11/15/98	Lima Peaks area, S. of Dillon, MT	1	1 hunter caught, buried, and killed
11/14/98	Yoho National Pk., British Columbia	1	6 hikers caught, some injured, 1 killed
11/13/98	Kokanee Glacier Provincial Pk., BC	1	6 caught in 2 separate avalanches; 1 missing and presumed drowned
11/7/98	Mt. Baldy, Utah	1	5 snowboarders caught; 1 killed, 1 seriously injured
6/11/98	Mount Rainier, Washington	1	12 climbers caught; 5 injured, 1 killed
5/31/98	Mount Hood, Oregon	1	4 climbers caught; 3 injured, 1 killed
5/17/98	Jasper, Alberta	1	1 snowboarder caught, buried, and killed

Date	Location	Deaths	Description
4/26/98	Denali National Park, Alaska	1	1 snowmobiler caught, buried, and killed
4/23/98	Provo Canyon, Utah	0	1 hiker caught twice; long rides; very lucky
4/20/98	Watson Lake, Yukon	1	teacher doing forest research caught and killed
4/20/98	Thompson Pass, Alaska	1	2 heli-skiers caught; 1 killed
4/19/98	Berthoud Pass, Colorado	1	2 snowboarders injured; 1 died later
4/1/98	St. Marys Glacier, Colorado	1	2 climbers caught; 1 buried and killed
3/29/98	Silverton, Colorado	0	cabin destroyed with man inside
3/26/98	Scotch Bonnett Peak, Montana	0	1 snowmobiler caught and buried
3/8/98	Aspen, Colorado	1	1 out-of-bounds skier caught, buried, and killed
3/7/98	Little Cottonwood Canyon, Utah	0	7 cars and 1 bus caught; 6 people injured
3/7/98	High Eastern Arctic	1	Unknown
3/1/98	Berthoud Pass, Colorado	1	2 caught; 1 backcountry skier and 1 snowboarder buried and killed
2/26/98	Little Cottonwood Canyon, Utah	0	cars caught; 2 people injured
2/22/98	Mormon Hills, Idaho	1	1 snowmobiler caught, buried, and killed
2/11/98	Donner Pass, California	1	1 snowboarder caught, buried, and killed
2/1/98	Barkerville, British Columbia	1	1 snowmobiler caught, buried, and killed
1/31/98	Grandview, Alaska	0	9 train coal cars caught; 3 derailed
1/29/98	Big Mountain, Montana	0	1 skier caught and buried
1/25/98	Merritt, British Columbia	1	1 skier caught, buried, and killed
1/24/98	Inspiration Pass, Montana	1	1 snowmobiler caught, buried, and killed
1/21/98	Lizard Head Pass, Colorado	1	1 snowboarder caught, buried, and killed
1/19/98	Cooke City, Montana	3	3 snowmobilers caught, buried, and killed
1/18/98	Blewett Pass, Washington	1	1 snowmobiler caught, buried, and killed
1/18/98	Sage Peak, Montana	1	1 snowmobiler caught, buried, and killed
1/18/98	Spring Canyon, Utah	1	1 snowmobiler caught, buried, and killed
1/17/98	Pleasant Creek, Utah	1	1 snowmobiler caught, buried, and killed
1/16/98	Elk Meadows, Utah	0	8 Boy Scouts caught; 4 fully buried, 4 partly buried
1/15/98	Sun Valley, Idaho	0	1 skier caught and buried
1/12/98	Solitude, Utah	0	1 skier caught, buried, and injured
1/11/98	Encampment, Wyoming	1	1 snowmobiler caught, buried, and killed
1/11/98	Rock Creek, Montana	0	1 snowmobiler caught and buried; very lucky
1/11/98	Little Cottonwood Canyon, Utah	4[+]	1 skier caught, buried, & injured; killed during evacuation in helicopter crash along with 3 aircrew members
1/10/98	Norns Creek, British Columbia	1	1 snowmobiler caught, buried, and killed
1/3/98	Island Park, Idaho	1	1 snowmobiler presumed caught, buried, and killed
1/3/98	Mission Mountains, Montana	1	1 snowshoer caught, buried, and killed
1/3/98	Shadow Lake, Montana	1	3 or 4 snowmobilers caught and buried; 1 killed
1/3/98	Island Park, Idaho	1	1 snowmobiler caught, buried, and killed
1/2/98	Kokanee Glacier, British Columbia	6	6 skiers caught, buried, and killed
1/2/98	New Denver, British Columbia	2	2 skiers caught, buried, and killed
1/2/98	Elliot Lake, British Columbia	4	4 snowmobilers caught and buried; 1 killed
12/30/97	Guanella Pass, Colorado	1	1 snowshoer caught, buried, and killed
12/29/97	Thompson Pass, Alaska	0	2 skiers caught; 1 fully and 1 partly buried
12/21/97	Hasler Flats, British Columbia	1	3 snowmobilers caught and buried; 1 killed
11/29/97	Canmore, Alberta	4	4 hikers caught, buried, and killed
11/24/97	Crow Pass, Alaska	1	1 hiker caught, buried, and killed
11/22/97	Tony Grove, Utah	0	2 snowboarders caught; 1 fully and 1 partly buried
11/9/97	Hatcher Pass, Alaska	1	2 snowboarders caught; 1 buried and killed

*as of April 30, 1999
[+]Indirectly related avalanche deaths

Courtesy of the Colorado Avalanche Information Center

Chapter 3

What Can Cause an Avalanche?

Snow on a slope is always in a tug-of-war. What holds a snow slab in place? The bonds between snow grains. What pulls snow downhill? Gravity.

An avalanche happens when stress (from gravity) exceeds strength (from bonds in snow). A snow slab will stay put only if forces holding it are greater than forces pulling it.

The snowpack can take a big strain without avalanching. That is if stress is applied slowly. Think of chewing gum on a cold day. The gum will stretch if pulled slowly. But it will break if rushed.

The ingredients of an avalanche are

1. a steep slope

2. a snowpack

3. a weak layer in the snowpack

4. a trigger

A stress can be a lot of snow falling on the snowpack. Or wind piling more snow on top. Or a skier, a snowboarder, an animal. These stresses can trigger an avalanche.

NATURAL TRIGGERS

A trigger is an event that starts an avalanche. Snowfall can trigger avalanches. Rain and rapid warming can too. These are natural triggers. A **natural avalanche** killed Doug Hall.

JANUARY 25, 1997. PROVO CANYON, UTAH. Doug Hall and Scott Lee were ice climbers. They were climbing a frozen waterfall. It was raining. Heavy snow was falling farther up the mountain. The rain soaked the new snow.

Above the ice climb, rain-weakened snow let loose. A small avalanche swept Doug and Scott off the ice. They fell over 300 feet straight down. Snow partly buried them.

Three other climbers saw it. They called 911 on their cell phone. Then they rushed to help. Doug did not respond to CPR. The Utah County Sheriff rescue crew arrived about 45 minutes after the accident. Members of the Sundance Ski Patrol also helped. But Doug Hall was dead. Scott Lee was badly injured.

This avalanche was caused by a natural trigger. But most avalanches that catch people are triggered by the victim or someone in the group.

SNOW TRAVELERS AS TRIGGERS

Most avalanche accidents are triggered by snow travelers. A coyote or an elk can set off a snowslide. So can people and their actions. Snowshoeing. Skiing. Snowmobiling. Snowboarding. Ice climbing. These can trigger an avalanche.

A CLOSE CALL

JANUARY 25, 1997. BIG COTTONWOOD CANYON, UTAH.
Cammille Coyle was snowshoeing with a friend. It was snowing hard. The new snow formed a soft slab. The slab lay on top of snow that was very different. The layers were not well-bonded. The heavy snowfall was triggering many small avalanches.

The two snowshoers were in a deep V-shaped gully. Cammille was in the lead. Suddenly her steps triggered a slide. The **soft-slab avalanche** came from above her. Cammille's partner was farther behind. She was not caught. Because it was in such a narrow gully, the small avalanche buried Cammile deeply.

Cammille's partner searched for her. Other skiers came upon the scene. They helped search. They contacted 911. Soon a Search and Rescue team arrived.

The rescuers dug in the debris. They poked the snow with poles called *probes*. Finally, a probe poked Cammille. They quickly dug her out. She was still alive and conscious. It seemed impossible!

Rescuers got her into dry clothes. They helped her walk. She made it almost to the main road. Then a rescue sled arrived. She took the ride.

Buried in snow, Cammille had been able to move her head back and forth. She made a big air pocket.

Half of completely buried avalanche victims suffocate within the first 30 minutes. About 25 percent are alive after the first hour. Very few are recovered alive.

Cammille was totally buried under six feet of snow. She was buried for over one and a half hours. And she lived through it!

EXPLOSIVES AS TRIGGERS: AVALANCHE CONTROL

Often the best way to prevent a deadly snowslide is to trigger one before it becomes a problem. This is called **avalanche control.** It is done with explosives. The rescue crew at Snowstorm Peak did this. They triggered avalanches from the air. After the snowslides, the slopes were safe for searchers.

Many ski resorts trigger safe avalanches. Snowbird is a big ski resort in Utah. It needs to stay safe for skiers. That's the job of Liam Fitzgerald. He oversees avalanche safety at Snowbird Resort.

Liam says, "Snowbird Resort has nearly 500 avalanche starting zones. Before daylight, we go out and perform snow-stability tests. If there's a hazard, we use explosives to release the avalanche. Experts throw **hand charges** into known starting zones. The hand-charge teams ski close enough to throw. But some areas are too remote or too dangerous for hand-charge teams. Then we fire **artillery.**"

Who's in charge of the artillery? The National Avalanche Center (NAC). The NAC is part of the U.S. Forest Service. The NAC is in charge of military weapons used for avalanche control.

Doug Abromeit manages the artillery program at

the NAC. He explains, "Military guns are used all over the west. The guns are in the mountains. They stay in locations experts can get to. The guns can shoot up to ten miles. Each shell weighs 40 to 50 pounds. They make a huge bang when they go off. Gun crews shoot shells into avalanche starting zones, deep in the mountains. Only well-trained operators do this."

KEEPING PEOPLE SAFE

Utah has many avalanches. The town of Alta, Utah, is right in an avalanche path.

Alta and nearby Snowbird are big ski areas. Avalanche control is important for towns like Alta. It's important for ski resorts like Snowbird. It's important along mountain highways. People driving on highways need to be safe from snowslides.

Some of the most experienced "snow folks" work for the highway department. Steve Conger is one of them. Steve is an avalanche **forecaster** in Utah. His home is in Alta.

Steve Conger watches the weather every day. He knows where avalanches happen. Each day he looks at the slide paths. Is there any new activity? He looks at the snowpack. Where is it weak? He digs snow pits in avalanche paths. How stable is the snowpack? Steve pokes the different layers. He breaks snow apart with a shovel. He takes the snow's temperature in many places. He looks at snow with a magnifying glass. If it storms, Steve studies the snow. All this helps answer one question: How likely is an avalanche?

Forecasters like Steve use all the facts. They rate the **avalanche hazard,** or risk of avalanche. Forecasters tell the Forest Service when to shoot the weapons. "In winter, this can happen two or three times a month," says Steve. "In some winters, it's two or three times a week."

All over the world, forecasters rate avalanche hazards. They all use the same scale: low, moderate, considerable, high, and extreme.

What keeps avalanche control safe? Experts are in charge. They plan when to set off avalanches. They make sure no people are near. In Alta, a phone network calls everyone. They tell people to stay indoors. They say, "Don't leave until we call you back." The highway is closed. No skiers are allowed on slopes.

Then the gun crews go up to the gun locations. They work very early, before daylight. They shoot the guns at the chosen target points. The avalanches run. When the snow stops, crews plow the roads. The phone net tells people it's safe to come out.

Avalanche control saves lives. Steve Conger reminds us, "Snow-covered ground looks smooth and inviting. But changing weather makes snow stronger or weaker. Knowing what makes snow weak is the key to understanding avalanches. It is the key to staying safe."

Chapter 4

For Safety's Sake

Many avalanche accidents can be avoided. You would not cross a highway without looking and listening. Anyone traveling on or near steep, snow-covered slopes needs to be just as careful.

Snow travelers must ask the right questions *before* they go and *as* they travel.

- Is this **avalanche terrain?**

- Could the snow slide?

- Is the weather making snow less stable?

- What are my choices?

TIP-OFFS TO DANGER

People on steep, snowy slopes need to *think*. They need to size up the avalanche hazard. Most accidents are the predictable outcome of a series of related events. People need to see when events are starting to stack up and work against them. Safe or unsafe? How can you know?

THE AVALANCHE TRIANGLE

Avalanches are formed by three factors. Weather. Terrain. Snowpack. These are known as the **avalanche triangle.**

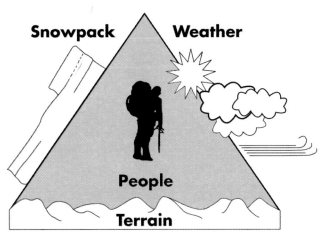

WEATHER. As soon as snow is on the ground, weather changes it. Weather makes the snowpack more stable or less stable. Wise snow travelers think about recent weather. And they watch for weather changes.

Weather can change fast. Safe can quickly become unsafe. Strong winds. New snowfall. Melting or rain. Big changes in temperature. All these affect avalanche danger.

AVALANCHE TERRAIN. Some terrain is not steep enough for an avalanche to happen. Any steep, snow-filled slope can be an avalanche path. It does not have to be a large, obvious path. Valley bottoms are not always safe. Look at the slopes above!

Slope angle is the most important feature. How steep is it? Snow on steeper slopes has more stress. Most slab avalanches happen on slopes with angles of 30 to 45 degrees. But they can also occur on steeper and less steep slopes. Many mountain travelers carry **compasses** with slope meters. They

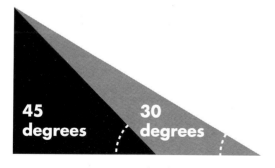

45 degrees

30 degrees

measure slope angles. Measuring is safer than guessing. It can help you be more certain if a slope can avalanche.

CUT YOUR RISKS

These are tips for finding safe mountain routes.

- In hazardous conditions, stick to tree stands, ridges, and low-angle slopes.

- Stay on slopes of 25 degrees or less. Make sure there are no steeper slopes above them.

- Travel at the valley floor. Stay away from large avalanche runouts.

- Travel along ridge tops, above avalanche paths, but avoid cornices.

- Go in dense timber. Trees help anchor the snow to steep slopes. This might keep avalanches from starting.

- Stay away from terrain traps like ravines. Even small amounts of snow could bury you deeply.

- Call the local avalanche advisory hot line for facts.

CUT YOUR RISKS

People can cut risks other ways too.

- Wear a **beacon.** Carry a shovel and collapsible probe pole.

- Don't go alone.

- Stay off steep slopes during and shortly after a storm. Let the snowpack settle at least 24 hours or longer.

- Go one person at a time when climbing up, down, or across avalanche areas. Going in groups leaves no one to dig you out if the snow slides.

- Drive only one snowmobile at a time on a steep slope. Many accidents happen when one machine gets stuck and another comes to help. Imagine the stress on the snowpack: two machines, two people!

Smart snow travelers watch for avalanche activity. Most large avalanche paths are easy to see. They are open slopes or bowls. Bent or damaged trees are also signs. These signs show where avalanches run.

SNOWPACK. How can you tell if snow is stable or not? Nature often gives clear clues. Fresh avalanches are the best clue. Snow that cracks is unstable. Snow that collapses is unstable. Snow that makes hollow sounds is also unstable.

The snowpack is made up of many different snow layers. Some layers are soft and fluffy. Others are hard. And some can be crusty and icy. These different layers sometimes do not bond to one another. Many unlike layers create a greater chance of avalanche.

Smart snow travelers learn the secrets of the snowpack. They learn how to read the layers. They dig snow pits about six feet deep. They study the layers. Hard layers above soft layers mean strong layers above weak layers. Snow travelers often look for loose, sugarlike snow. Such snow is a poor, weak base for layers above. This makes a snowpack unstable—just right for avalanches.

No one can stop an avalanche. But experts say nearly all avalanche accidents can be avoided. One key is reading nature's tip-offs to danger. Another key is **route finding**—choosing the safest route.

Chances are slim for someone buried in an avalanche. Only one-third of totally buried victims survive.

Only one victim in three will survive burial after one hour. One in six after two hours. And one in ten after three hours.

In the U.S., 22 hours is the longest someone was buried and still lived. It was the miner, Lester Morlang, buried in Colorado on November 17, 1985.

WHAT IF YOU GET CAUGHT?

Imagine you are skiing. You hear a woomph. *Avalanche!* A chunk of snow the size of a riding lawnmower knocks you down. You're caught in the slide. What should you do?

CUT YOUR RISKS

People can cut risks other ways too.

- Be sure your group knows how to use the equipment.

- Cross a slope at the very top or bottom.

- Never enter the slope above your buddy. If the snow slides, it could bury him or her.

- Dig snow pits and study the layers. Change plans if you need to.

- Climb and descend at the edge of a slope, not the center.

- Plan an escape route, just in case. This may save you if a slab breaks loose. Look for an island of safety. Ridges, big trees, and low slopes all work.

- Take classes in avalanche awareness.

33

If You're Caught in an Avalanche

1. Yell! Get someone's attention.

2. Try to escape to the side. Or grab a tree or a rock.

3. Get rid of your poles and skies. Swim with the avalanche. Try to stay on top.

4. Fight the avalanche. Flail your arms and kick your legs.

5. As the avalanche slows down, try to get your hands in front of your face to create an air pocket.

6. If you're near the surface, thrust up your arm. Your hand may mark where you are. Rescuers can see it.

7. Do anything to make an air space.

8. Try to break out of the snow. If you can't clear your head fast, stop trying. Be still and conserve oxygen.

9. Yell only when you hear rescuers nearby. Snow is a good conductor of sound. But wind or noises may make it hard for rescuers to hear your yells.

PROTECTION: AVALANCHE RESCUE GEAR

Today there's help to find a buried victim. It's an avalanche beacon, or **transceiver.** This is a small, battery-powered device. You wear it against your body, under clothing. When turned on, it gives a constant signal.

Everyone in the group wears their beacon on "transmit." If someone gets buried, the others switch to "receive." They can hear the signal from the buried person. They can find and rescue him or her.

A beacon is the best tool for finding a buried victim. Only one of three victims buried without a beacon survives. Even people who ski alone should wear one. It could save rescuers hours of searching.

Avalanche balloon systems are the latest safety gear. The balloon acts like an air bag. You wear it in a backpack. It inflates when you pull a cord.

When used during an avalanche, it "floats" the trapped person. You stay near the top of the snow. Its bright color helps rescuers see you.

Dale Atkins of the Colorado Avalanche Information Center explains how it works. "Imagine a bowl of mixed nuts. When you pick up the bowl, you don't see the big nuts. So you shake the bowl. Small nuts settle downward, forcing big nuts to the top.

"There's a lot of shaking in an avalanche. Forward, up, and down. Any big objects are forced to the top of the snow. There they stay. The avalanche air bag was developed in the late 1970s by a German forester. He saw that large trees stayed on top of avalanche debris piles. That gave him the idea."

The air bags work great. The problem is the cost. A basic model in the United States is about $1,200. Few people can afford it. They are more common in Europe.

Shovels and probes are important gear too. An avalanche

shovel is used for digging out a buried victim. Shovels can be used to dig snow pits too.

Avalanche probes look like tent poles. People use probes to poke around for victims. Probes can pinpoint avalanche victims found with a beacon. Then rescuers know right where to dig.

SAVED BY A BEACON

MARCH 9, 1997. LOGAN, UTAH. Three backcountry skiers were skiing. They were in a steep canyon. Four dogs were along. On their third run, disaster struck. The first skier triggered a slab two feet thick. It took him for a 2,500-foot vertical ride. He was totally buried. His friends were also caught above him. Luckily, they were able to stop their slide.

The friends located the victim using a beacon. It took less than 20 minutes. He was blue and not breathing. They gave him mouth-to-mouth. He breathed but did not "wake up." He had a head injury. One dog was also lost, buried in the slide.

A passing snowmobiler had a cell phone. He called Cache County Search and Rescue (SAR). The victim was flown to an Ogden hospital in serious condition.

RIDING THE "WHITE TIGER"

MARCH 11, 1997. ASPEN, COLORADO. Two Aspen snowboarders met trouble. One rider triggered a small avalanche. He was caught. His friend could only watch him "riding the white tiger." There was no way to help.

At first, he thought the slide did not seem like much. But not for long. The wet snowslide grew as it slid. It grew to about 40 feet across. It seemed like quicksand. The snowboarder could not escape.

The avalanche swept toward the trees. It slammed him along. It was like being in a cement mixer. The avalanche broke trees. It ripped his snowboard from his boots. But that helped. With his feet free, he could swim with the avalanche. He rode about 500 feet. The avalanche slowed. He grabbed a tree with his legs. It finally stopped.

The second snowboarder hurried down. He helped his injured friend. The victim used the avalanche shovels as small crutches. They hobbled to the road and their car. Then they drove to the hospital.

The victim was lucky. His helmet and his backpack likely saved his life. During the avalanche he hit trees with his back and head. Yet he was able to walk away from the "white tiger." He made a complete recovery.

EXPECT THE UNEXPECTED

Dale Atkins (CAIC) wrote the accident report for this snowboarder. He said, "This incident showed the importance of wearing a helmet. We tend not to think of helmets when skiing and snowboarding.

"The pair were well equipped. They carried avalanche rescue gear. But they were not expecting trouble. The victim rode the same line 12 to 15 times this season. Just the day before, he rode a different line. But it was similar in **elevation** and steepness."

Dale points out two mistakes. First, it does not matter how many times you've gone down a steep slope in the past. Past actions tell nothing of today's stability. Especially during springlike conditions. Second, the pair didn't recognize changing snow conditions. This skill builds with time spent in the mountains. It takes a long time to learn how things work together to change snow stability.

Dale says, "Even when you are certain of avalanche conditions, expect the unexpected."

Avalanche Hot Lines

You have your beacon. You have your gear. Now call the hot line. Learn the current conditions before you go.

In Colorado, seven hot lines carry recorded messages. Other mountain states have them too. They tell weather, snow, and avalanche conditions. These are updated at least once a day. Mountain radio stations broadcast the hot line messages daily.

These facts help in planning. But snow travelers need to beware. Once in the backcountry, conditions may have changed. Then plans may need to change. The most important thing isn't riding the steepest slope. Or making the first tracks. The most important thing is staying alive. Then you can do it again.

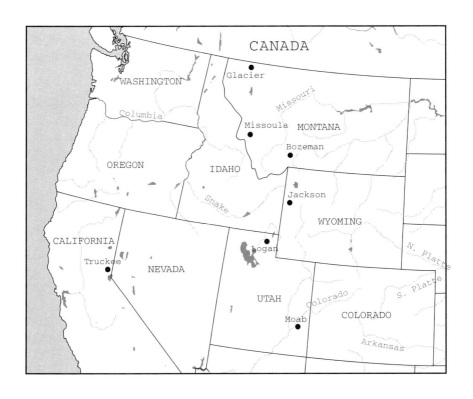

Avalanche Information Centers

Avalanche Information Centers have hot lines. These centers have Internet sites. They offer classes. They train avalanche experts. They do avalanche forecasting and control. Avalanche Information Centers in North America are

- Moab, Utah
- Logan, Utah
- Jackson, Wyoming
- NW Montana (Glacier)
- Missoula, Montana

- SW Montana (Bozeman)
- Colorado
- Truckee, California
- Canada

Studying Avalanches

Avalanches have been happening for thousands of years. People have figured out how to trigger them. They have

triggered safe avalanches to prevent accidental ones. They even have triggered avalanches in wars.

During World War II, enemy troops from Austria and Italy faced each other across huge mountains. They did not bomb the enemy. They aimed their bombs at the snowy slopes. Then avalanches did the killing.

THE SWISS FEDERAL INSTITUTE FOR SNOW AND AVALANCHE RESEARCH

We know how avalanches start. We know how to trigger them. But can we prevent them? There's still a lot to learn.

Many people live near Europe's giant Alps. Their homes are in the shadows of high mountains. These people love snow.

But they know it can turn deadly. They are trained to stay alert. They know the signs of trouble in the snow. They know when the slopes are unstable. And they're prepared to deal with it.

Preventing avalanches is the way to save lives. That's the mission of the Swiss Federal Institute for Snow and Avalanche Research.

Here, avalanche forecasting is high tech. Scientists at the Institute study the structure of snow. They find new ways of predicting and surviving avalanches. They study how snow behaves. That's the key to predicting avalanches.

The scientists study snow in a cold lab. Here they can deal with their subject in a controlled place. The lab is chilled to below-zero temperatures. They slice and study snow samples from all over Switzerland.

They study snow to see how strong it is. They put a snow sample in a machine. This machine acts like gravity. Gravity is the ultimate cause of every avalanche. The machine gives clues to the forces that hold snow together, or make it give way.

INSIDE AN AVALANCHE

We know the basic causes of avalanches. But there's much more to learn. In Switzerland, scientists study avalanches from the inside. They work from within a concrete **bunker** on a steep slope. The "house" is built to withstand a direct hit. Then they trigger an avalanche. Radar tells them the avalanche speed. Steel shutters slam shut two seconds before the snow hits. The force is 1,000 pounds per square inch.

It is scary for people in the test bunker. But they learn more about avalanches. They think of skiers in the path of an avalanche. Those skiers have *nothing* between them and a crushing wave of snow.

PROTECTION FROM AVALANCHES

Through the years, the Swiss have learned a lot. Many homes in the Alps are protected by steel shutters. They may have stone walls. Roads are covered by **snowsheds**. These provide safe routes through mountain passes.

There are hundreds of miles of special fences. The fences are built on mountainsides across the country. They help slow avalanches before they reach towns below. All these ways are taught to younger generations. And they keep learning more.

Chapter 6

Search and Rescue (SAR)

Avalanche victims can sometimes dig themselves out. Lester Morlang did. Or sometimes people with the victim can do the rescue.

Liam Fitzgerald says, "The best hope for survival is if someone sees where you're buried. They can find a ski or hand or hat and recover you quickly. That doesn't always happen. Sometimes people are buried and there's no sign.

"If you have to depend on an organized rescue, it can be 15 minutes in a ski resort—or 4 hours in backcountry—before help arrives. Most skiers don't use beacons. So the next best thing is a trained avalanche rescue dog. But even the best trained crew has to be told. Then they have to get there. It takes time."

By the time a rescue crew gets there, time has usually run out for the victim.

About 90 percent of avalanche victims are alive after 15 minutes. But at 30 minutes, less than 50 percent are alive. After 2 hours, it's only between 8 and 16 percent. Speedy rescues are critical.

PERCENT SURVIVAL VERSUS BURIAL TIME

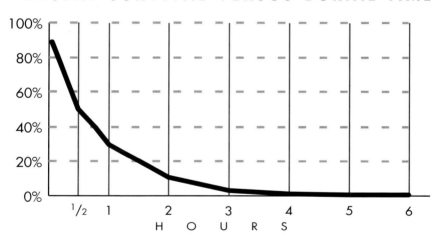

| T Y P E | O F | R E S C U E | |
	Self Rescue	Found by Party Members	Found by Organized Rescue Team	Total
Alive	45	170	56	271
Dead		40	272	344
	45	210	328	615

1950/51 to 1996/97   Colorado Avalanche Information Center

Stay and Search or Go for Help?

The faster the rescue, the better the chances. The first 15 minutes are the most crucial for saving a life. If there's a snowslide, remember what experts say. *It is best never to leave the site.* Look for signs of the victim. A hand or a ski might be showing. If you have found nothing and must leave, take a good look around. Mark where you last saw the victim. If you go for help, you will most likely come back to find a body.

February 12, 1997. British Columbia, Canada. Three snowboarders were at a ski resort. They decided to cross a ridge and ski outside boundaries.

The first person down dropped into a gully below the ridge. This triggered a small avalanche. That triggered a huge slab release. The bigger avalanche swept the skier to the bottom of the slope. Her two friends didn't see her. They didn't try to reach her.

But they heard her yelling. They went to find help.

Soon, experts from the resort came. A rescue unit came. They followed the avalanche path to the bottom. They saw no sign of the victim. Not in the path. Not at the snow pile. But they found footprints. The tracks led down to a creek. There were no signs that the person was hurt.

Then they found her. She was lying in a small creek. She had slipped and fallen. Her head hit rocks in the creek. Cause of death was not the avalanche. She walked away from that. She died from head injuries and freezing—events *after* the avalanche. That's when her friends were gone, in search of help.

AVALANCHE RESCUE DOGS

Dogs can be great searchers. Search dogs were first used in Europe. Larger breeds, like St. Bernards, were favored. They could break trail through deep snow. These days, handlers often have to lift their dogs up the mountain. Dogs share a chairlift or a snowmobile ride. Or they ride in a helicopter. Medium-size dogs are better for this. They can also move quickly over the snow without wallowing.

Liam Fitzgerald says, "Most ski resorts with avalanche problems have rescue dogs. Snowbird Resort has four avalanche rescue dogs. Dogs can move quicker than people during a search."

There are many search-dog and handler teams. Dog teams are often called first. Dogs can cover large areas faster than people.

Rescue work is team work. There are many kinds of teams. One is Explorer Search and Rescue (ESAR). This is a Boy Scout organization. There are the Mountain Rescue Association and ski patrol teams. All teams count on many other experts— helicopters, non-ESAR ground teams, ham radio clubs, people with four-wheel-drive vehicles. These are just a few who help in SAR (search and rescue).

Dan and Cooper: A Rescue Team

Dan Comden does SAR work. Like most rescuers, Dan is a volunteer. His partner is Cooper, a golden retriever. Dan grew up with search-and-rescue dogs in his family. He tells about rescue dogs.

"The dogs need to have the drive to find the lost person. Most dogs develop what we call a strong penetration drive. That's where they dig to where the person is or where the scent's coming from. That's when they get their reward. When the person's uncovered. Some dogs are so focused it's hard to get them out of the way so shovelers can clear the area.

"Rescue dogs like Cooper wear orange vests. These identify a working dog. That's important when the dog is working in a ski area. Or in a national park where dogs aren't usually allowed **off-lead.** Some dogs wear a lift harness. This helps in rescues using chairlifts or helicopters."

The safety of all the searchers is important. Dan says, "Teams ask for backup experts. They don't want any more victims. Before they go into the slide area, they test each other's beacons. They make sure they're working right."

For avalanche-search qualification, handlers study many things. They study snow travel, avalanche beacons and other tools, avalanche safety, search techniques, and terrain evaluation. They learn first aid for people and for dogs. Dan says the handlers need more training than the dogs.

Rescue Dog at Work

For 20 years, the backcountry around Sun Valley had no skiing deaths from avalanches. Not until January 5, 1996. The avalanche advisory was good. The danger was moderate to low at all elevations. So what went wrong?

Two brothers and a friend set out for fun. One brother skied ahead. The other two boys carried their snowboards. They walked along a road to a slope for snowboarding. The slope above the road was very steep. The two walked side by side. The weight of two bodies was too much. It triggered a **hard-slab avalanche.**

The hard slab released above them. The slide swept them downhill toward rocks and trees. It was not a huge slide. But no one was wearing an avalanche beacon. No one had a shovel. Because of this, the partner on skis could not rescue them. He had not seen where the snowslide took his buddies. He went for help.

One hour after the slide, a rescue helicopter landed. Shelby arrived. He was an avalanche-rescue dog. He came with a heli-guide and three Ski Patrols. Within 15 minutes of landing, Shelby had found the victims.

It was too late. One hour and twenty minutes had passed since the avalanche. The boys had suffocated under the snow. Shelby's search was good. But it came too late.

Chapter

Not All Bad: The Upside of Avalanches

Death and disaster. Towns buried. Roads destroyed. Trees and skiers scraped off mountains. These are results of snowslides. How could snowslides bring any good? It seems unlikely. Yet, new research says there *is* some good.

Avalanches can give as well as take. Avalanches create habitats for many plants and animals. Caribou, wolverines, small mammals, birds, and grizzly bears are examples. How can this be?

Avalanches travel the same routes each winter. The snowslides keep slopes free of trees. Then more sunlight

reaches the ground. The slides clean off much of the snow. The tops of plants and shrubs can stick up through the snow that's left. Other plants can grow there too. This is easy food for animals to find.

The woods around the avalanche paths may lie under ten feet of snow. Elk, moose, deer, and mountain goats have a hard time finding food. It is hard for them to walk in such deep snow.

Avalanche paths can help grazing animals survive the winter. Animals can trot out to eat. They eat the plant tops that can grow in open chutes but not in the shady woods.

In spring, the paths also help. Shallow snow melts faster. New plant life grows sooner. Caribou come to graze. Grizzlies eat flower bulbs in the meadows made by an avalanche. Birds, wolverines, and small mammals find food there too.

Not all animals are grazers. Meat eaters cruise the avalanche debris piles. They will feed on other animals killed in avalanches. Wolverines may den in the boulders and downed trees at the bottom of the chute. They can feed on caribou, mountain goats, elk, or deer who die in the snowslides.

Experts studied grizzlies near Glacier National Park. Here, avalanche paths make up only five percent of the landscape. Yet bears spend more than half their time there. They eat, rest, and breed in the chute area. Many return to the same slide year after year.

Canada's Columbia River basin has many avalanche paths. In summer, dozens of bird species nest and feed there. Many birds nest in holes. They flock to the old trees often found along slides. Such trees should be left for birds to live in.

Wildlife experts want avalanche paths protected. They call them **buffer zones.** The habitat created in buffer zones helps wildlife. Chutes are also natural fire breaks. They help to stop wildfires. When paths are left as buffer zones, the deadly slides help give back life.

Glossary

artillery	military guns used to trigger avalanches as far away as ten miles
atmosphere	the mass of air surrounding the earth
avalanche	a snowslide moving suddenly and swiftly down a mountain; can also be mud, ice, or rock slides
avalanche balloon system	a safety device that inflates from a pack to keep an avalanche victim on top of the snowslide
avalanche control	any measure taken to control the size and frequency of avalanches or to direct the path of an avalanche
avalanche debris	the ice, dirt, rock, trees, or other junk found where an avalanche stops
avalanche hazard	the risk of an avalanche
avalanche path	the entire area down which an avalanche moves; made up of the starting zone, track, and runout zone
avalanche terrain	any terrain in which avalanches occur (e.g., steep slopes and gullies)
avalanche track	the middle part of an avalanche path below the starting zone and above the runout zone; also called chute
avalanche triangle	the three things needed for an avalanche— weather, terrain, snowpack

backcountry	areas outside developed ski areas
beacon	an electronic device snow travelers can wear to help them be found in case of an avalanche; also called a transceiver
blizzard	a long, severe snowstorm
bond	to cause two layers of snow to hold together; what holds the layers of snow together
buffer zones	a protected avalanche path that helps wildlife
bunker	a protective shelter
buried	when an avalanche victim's head is under the snow after an avalanche stops, even if other parts are out of the snow
compass	device that shows direction
cornice	an overhanging mass of snow formed by wind-drifted snow over a ridge
elevation	height above sea level
forecast	ability to predict something such as the weather or possibility of an avalanche
hand charge	an explosive charge used in avalanche control. Hand carried to the control site and either thrown or planted in the snow before detonation.
hard-slab avalanche	an avalanche containing a hard slab or blocks of slab snow that hold their shape as the avalanche slides. It is difficult to even kick the toe of your boot into a hard slab.
high marking	contest where snowmobilers try to make the highest marks on a slope

loose-snow avalanche	when loose snow grains slide on a slope. They start from a point and gather more snow as they slide down.
natural avalanche	any avalanche that occurs without being triggered by active control, or that is not accidentally triggered by a snow traveler
off-lead	without a leash; running free
route finding	the process of safe travel around avalanche terrain
runout zone	where an avalanche slows and stops
slab	a well-bonded layer or layers of snow
snowpack	all the snow layers on the ground; snow cover
snowshed	huts along roads that offer travelers shelter in the event of an avalanche
snowslide	another name for an avalanche
soft-slab avalanche	an avalanche containing soft snow where the blocks break up as the avalanche slides. Soft slab can be good powder-skiing snow.
starting zone	where unstable snow breaks loose and an avalanche begins
timberline	highest point where trees grow on a mountain
transceiver	an electronic device snow travelers can wear to help them be found in case of an avalanche; also called a beacon
trigger	a force that starts an avalanche

Index